Everett Grist's
Machine-Made and Contemporary Marbles

Second Edition

COLLECTOR BOOKS

A Division of Schroeder Publishing Co., Inc.

The current values in this book should be used only as a guide. They are not intended to set prices, which vary from one section of the country to another. Auction prices as well as dealer prices vary greatly and are affected by condition as well as demand. Neither the Author nor the Publisher assumes responsibility for any losses that might be incurred as a result of consulting this guide.

Searching for a Publisher?

We are always looking for knowledgeable people considered to be experts within their fields. If you feel that there is a real need for a book on your collectible subject and have a large conprehensive collection, contact Collector Books.

Printed by IMAGE GRAPHICS, INC., Paducah, Kentucky

Thank You

A special thanks to the following collectors/dealers who have furnished pictures and/or advice which helped tremendously in putting this book together. They are buyers of good marbles and sometimes have marbles for sale.

An extra special thanks to Sally Dolly for her photographs of rare marbles, some of which are used here and in my other books.

Gary and Sally Dolly
P. O. Box 2044
New Smyrna Beach, FL 32170-2044
(904)428-4450

Brian Estepp
10380 Taylor Road SW
Reynoldsburg, OH 43068
(614)863-5350

Jim and Louise O'Connell
5309 Wright
Troy, MI 48098
(810)879-0438

Danny and Gretchen Turner
Running Rabbit Video Auctions
P.O. Box 701
Waverly, TN 37185
(615)296-3600

Marble Clubs

We highly recommend the following marble collector clubs. We suggest you contact them for information on membership and dates for upcoming marble collectors' conventions.

Marble Collector's Society of America
P.O. Box 222
Trumbull, CT 06611

Marble Collectors Unlimited
P.O. Box 206
Northboro, MA 01532

Buckeye Marble Collectors Club
437 Meadowbrook Drive
Newark, OH 43055

Southern California Marble Club
18361-1 Strothern Street
Reseda, CA 91335

Marbles

Machine-made marbles as the marble collectors speak of them today cover a wide variety of designs, produced over a long period of time from the early years of the twentieth century to the present time. The earliest machines were fairly simple, hand-fed and manually powered. Therefore, the earliest machine-made marbles were expensive compared to the clay, porcelain and hand-made marbles imported from Germany. The machines were constantly improved over the years, with the most important change coming about with the automatic feeder in about the late 1920's. Machine-made marbles should really be classed in two different groups: early machine-made marbles (1900 – 1925) and automatic machine-made marbles (1925 to the present); but it is not always possible to tell one from the other. Two types of the early machine-made marbles are easily recognized because of the design. They are the marbles that have the "6" or "9" in the design and the marbles that are called diaper folds by some collectors. Understanding the method of feeding the machine makes these types of marbles easily attributed to the early machine. This is explained fully in the book *M.F. Christensen and The Perfect Glass Ball Machine* by Michael C. Cohill.

The language of the marble collector is different and not easily understood by most other English-speaking people. Some words which are found in the dictionary mean something altogether different to the collector. Take, for instance, the word *pontil*. A pontil is a metal rod on which a "gather" of molten glass is held while shaping it into a desired object. A pontil mark is the rough spot left where the pontil rod was broken from the object upon completion. A ground pontil is when the rough spot has been smoothed by grinding. Therefore, in reality, the only marbles with pontil marks are those that have been shaped by hand on the end of a pontil rod. But the early hand-made marbles have long been referred to by the collector as having two pontils when really the rough spots were made by the marble scissors. Today, any imperfection in the machine-made marble is being referred to by some collectors as a pontil when actually a pontil rod was never used in the manufacturing process. Instead, a punty rod was used, the difference being a knob or ball on the end of the punty rod which kept the entire blob of molten glass from falling off at one time while the marble machine was being fed.

Another type of imperfection was caused by the expulsion of gasses from the body of the marble as it was cooling, leaving small bumps. When practical, these imperfections were polished by grinding or were fire-polished, while others were placed on the reject pile for later melting and re-use. One of the most common imperfections was a crease, caused when an amount of molten glass larger than the pathway of the machine could handle was fed into the machine. This is sometimes called a crease pontil. Is this not just a wee bit ridiculous?

I have no desire to change the language of the marble collector. Rather, the purpose of writing this is the hope for a better understanding among collectors of the terms being utilized. For a more thorough study, we suggest you read and use the "Glossary of Terms" of the Marble Collector's Society of America, which we hope will be slightly amended and greatly expanded in the future.

We like names for marbles rather than numbers and although the names we like best are those given to them by the manufacturer, we cannot always find names for them from that source. Our next-best source is the name used by the children "way back when," but this is sometimes confusing because names differed from region to region. The name we like least is that given by the modern-day collector; but let me hasten to say, any name in general used by the collectors is better than no name at all.

An example of a latter-day name is *diaper fold*. I don't believe a manufacturer would call one of his marbles a diaper fold or that an eight- to 14-year-old child would have dubbed a favorite marble a diaper fold. I suggest this name could only have been thought of by a young father marble collector who had been changing a lot of diapers.

Another example is the *hurricane*. When I asked from whence the name came, the reply was, "Doesn't this remind you of the hurricane pictured on the weather map on TV?" Well, this eliminates the name being one used by the manufacturer because the marbles are older than television itself.

I have read all the good books that I know of on marbles, including but not limited to those by Bauman, Randall and Webb, Castle, Cohill and Carskadden and I recommend that all marble collectors do likewise. However, my writings are based on experience and observation while buying and selling marbles for more than 10 years.

Plate I: Culet from the Akro Agate Clarksburg, West Virginia, site. Photo from *Collectors Encyclopedia of Akro Agate* by Gene Florence, courtesy of Gene Florence.

Plate 2: Culet from the Christensen Agate site in Cambridge, Ohio.

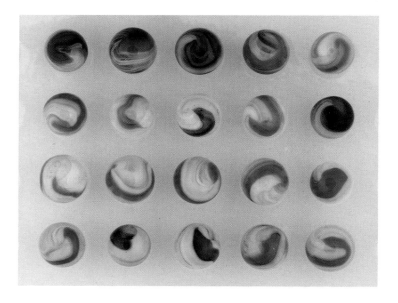

Plate 3: Popeyes all seem to be clear and white with two other colors of glass and are corkscrews. Four boxes are pictured in Plates 50 and 51 for the purpose of showing as many different marbles in the original boxes as possible. In corkscrew marbles, the marble design, a line or lines starting at one point of the marble, will go completely around at least one time without crossing or touching, in the manner of the common corkscrew. All corkscrews are attributed to the Akro Agate Company.

Plate 4: More Popeyes. On line 4, A and B are hybrid Popeyes. It is believed they were developed when the machine was being changed to different colors, resulting in more colors in the marble.

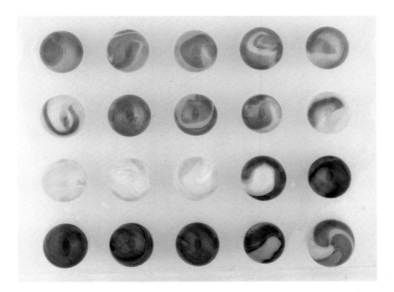

Plate 5: Marbles on line one are called limeade corkscrews. On line two are Akro Agate Imperials. In line three, A through C are called lemonade corkscrews; D is an opaque corkscrew; E is the Akro Agate carnelian agate. In line four, A through D are two-color opaque corkscrews; E is a tri-colored Akro Agate corkscrew. To see these marbles in the original boxes, check plates 52, 56, 68, and 69.

Plate 6: More corkscrews. Lines one, two, and four show tri-color corkscrews. Line three shows transparent corkscrews.

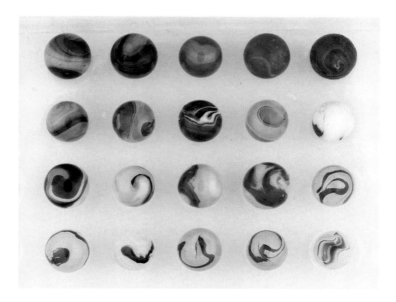

Plate 7: These are the now-famous Akro Agate marbles containing the oxblood color. Line one, A and B are carnelian agates. Rows C and D are bricks with white; E is the ordinary brick. Line two, A and B are the lemonade with oxblood; C is a brick with white; D is a lemonade corkscrew with a small line of oxblood; E is a white marble with oxblood. Line 3, A through D, are egg yolk and oxblood. The remaining marbles in the plate are silver oxbloods.

Plate 8: More oxbloods and bricks. Line one shows three carnelian oxbloods flanked by lemonade oxbloods. Line two has all blue oxbloods. Lines three and four show bricks.

Plate 9: These are all oxbloods. Line one are blue oxbloods. Line three are silver oxbloods. Lines two and four are a combination of egg yolk, lemonade, and limeade oxbloods.

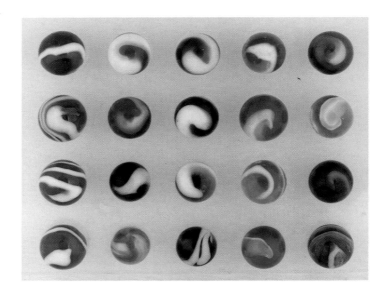

Plate l0: Akro Agate opaque white and transparent colored glass corkscrews.

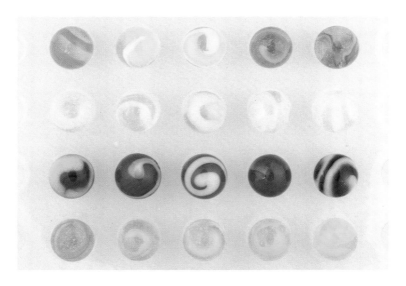

Plate ll: Lines one, two, and four are clear and transparent colored glass with the opaque ribbon corkscrew. Line three are opaque corkscrews.

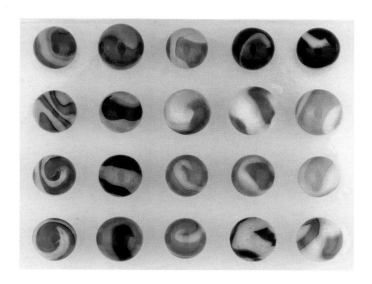

Plate 12: A variety of opaque glass corkscrews.

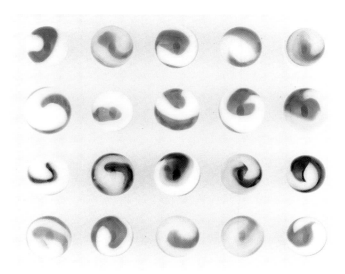

Plate 13: Akro Agate opaque white and colored corkscrews. Also see plate 63.

Plate 14: Akro Agate sparklers. This is a close-up of the marbles in plate 55. Also see plate 49. Courtesy Gary and Sally Dolly.

On the next page are shown some Christensen Agate marbels. We think they were made at this plant because of the unusual colors. Many of these colors are shown in the book *Cambridge Glass in Color* published by Collector Books of Paducah, Kentucky. I would advise collectors interested in these marbles to refer to this book, as much of the glass used by Christensen Agate was from the Cambridge Glass factory. Much can be learned from this book, one item in particular pertaining to pink marbles. The little pink marble that is making the rounds today is attributed to the Cambridge factory, and was supposedly produced from the Crown Tuscan pink glass. However, the Crown Tuscan glass was not manufactured until after the Christensen Agate plant had been closed. Though the marble factory was in operation only a relatively short time, about five years I believe, they produced some of the most beautiful marbles of the machine-made marble era. This was due, no doubt, to the fact that they used the discarded glass from the Cambridge Glass factory. It seems that a large number of these marbles have survived the passage of time, a fact I attribute to their being prized possessions of those who owned them.

Plate 15: Christensen Agate marbles. Line one are called turkeys. Lines two and three are called flames. Line four are hurricanes. Is this a joke, or what? Some of these marbles can be transposed from one name to another simply by showing a different side of the marble. Despite their names, they are all beautiful, as are most of the marbles attributed to the Christensen Agate Company of Cambridge, Ohio.

Plate 16: Christensen Agate marbles, miscellaneous and unusual examples. These were all purchased in the Cambridge, Ohio, area and are believed to have been produced by the Christensen Agate Company.

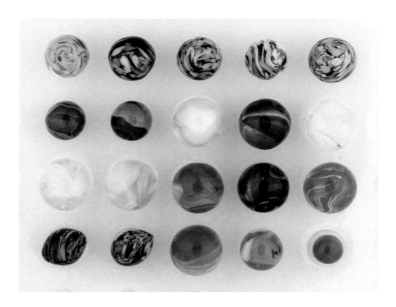

Plate 17: Christensen Agate marbles. Line one are guineas (see plate 86). Rows A and B in line two are called corals. These have been attributed by some people to the Peltier Glass Company of Ottawa, Illinois. I do not have positive proof but I have bought this type of marble from three different sources in the Cambridge, Ohio, area and the people who sold them to me attributed them to the Christensen Agate Company. The remaining three marbles in line two and those in line three are slags attributed to the Christensen Agate company. Line four, A and B, are guineas that did not come out right. The first one is the shape of a football, the second is in the shape of an egg. This seemed to have happened at the Cambridge plant often, for some reason or another. I have seen several supposed-to-have-been marbles in this shape. The remaining three marbles are slags. The fifth marble in the row is a green peewee.

Plate 18: Line one has clear base and blue base guineas, with a cyclone in the center. Line two shows two striped opaques, a coral swirl, and two two-color swirls. Line three has a bloodie on the left and the rest are flames. Line four is all striped opaques.

Plate 19: Lines one and two are guineas. In line three are cyclones. These are also referred to by some collectors as cobras or clearies. Lines four and five are flames. Courtesy of Brian Estepp.

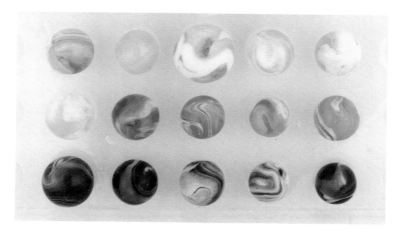

Plate 20: Slags. Because of the color of these marbles, we believe all to have been produced at the Christensen Agate Company of Cambridge, Ohio.

Plate 21: Comic marbles by Peltier. Peltier Glass Co. of Ottawa, Illinois, is another famous marble maker. Their most popular marble is the picture or "comic" marble. They also sold marbles under the names "National Rainbows" and "Champion Jr." Collectors have given certain colors common names and this has caught on, making them some of the most sought-after marbles on today's market.

Plate 22: Line one is called Superman. Line two is rebel. Line three is Christmas trees. Line four is ketchup & mustard. From the collection of Danny and Gretchen Turner.

Plate 23: All these are Peltier marbles. Line one center is a Christmas tree, the rest are liberties. Line two is Chrismas trees, line three is rebels. Line four starts out with a rose yellow base tricolor rainbow. Next is a blue base rainbow, two Supermans, and a ketchup & mustard.

Plate 24: A variety of later Peltier marbles. Many of those were sold under the name Champion Jr.

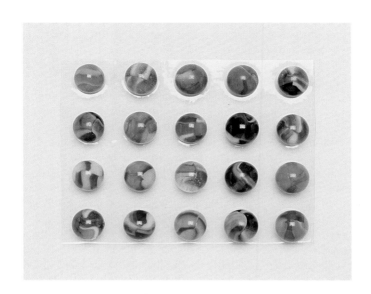

Plate 25: More Champion Jrs.

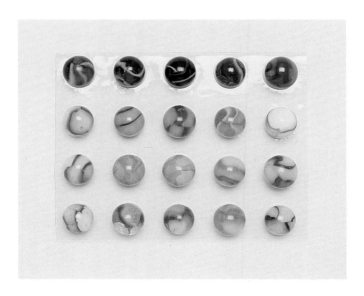

Plate 26: More Champion Jrs.

21

Slags

The major producers of slag marbles were Akro Agate, M.F. Christensen and Christensen Agate. Some of the Akros were sold in boxes labeled Carnelian Reds as shown in plate 46. Some of the Christensen Agates were sold as The World's Best Bloodies as pictured in plate 78. The M.F. Christensen slags were sold as follows: oxblood (brick) as American carnelian, green and amber as National Onyx, and then Blue Onyx, White Onyx and Purple Onyx.

We cannot be sure who made which but from my observation of marbles in boxes and pictures, I believe (as a general rule) marbles made by M.F. Christensen have more white than colored glass. Those made by Akro Agate contain more colored than white; and in marbles made by Christensen Agate, the transparent glass is much clearer than those of the other companies. This is due, no doubt, to the fact that Christensen Agate was located across the street from and used glass from the Cambridge Glass factory. Keep in mind that marbles were purchased by Akro Agate from both of the other companies and sold under their own label. One thing we can be sure of is that they are all slags and not Akro Agates, as claimed by some marble collectors a few years ago.

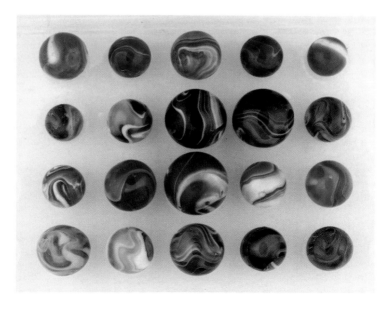

Plate 27: Slags.

Plate 28: Line one is '9' slags from M.F. Christensen & Son. Line two is from Christensen Agate, as are A and B in Line 3. The rest are from various manufacturers.

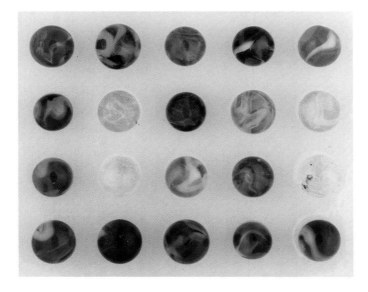

Plate 29: A different type of slag. All examples of this type of slag that I have found packaged were in boxes like the one in plate 100. Some of the boxes were red, some were blue. I have been told empty boxes were sold to stores which purchased marbles in bulk to fill the boxes; therefore, there is no company name on the box. I have been told by some of the older hardware and variety store operators that this was a common practice in the late 1940's and early 1950's.

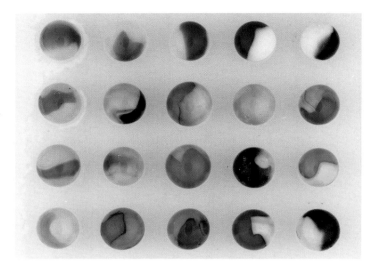

Plate 30: Row one are moss agates. The remaining rows are half-and-half marbles made by Akro Agate as well as other companies.

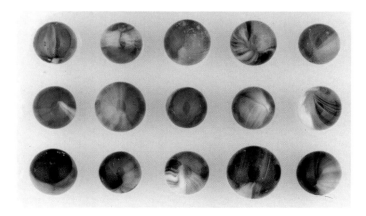

Plate 31: These are Master Made sunbursts mixed in with maybe one or two Akro Agate sparklers. See plate 97 for further identification.

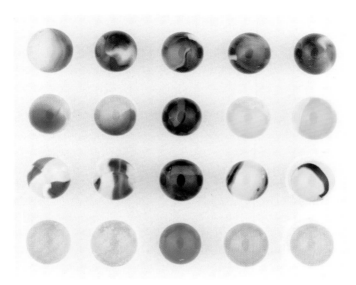

Plate 32: Moss agates, 7-ups, black widows, boy scouts and bumblebees. Line four are unusual examples of marbles that I have not often encountered. They are solid colors but look like the glass in moss agates.

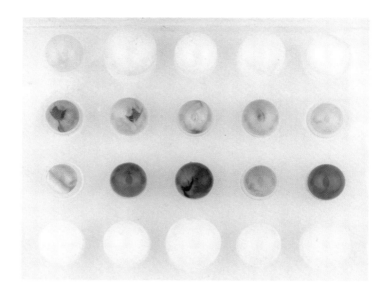

Plate 33: Line one are Akro Agate moonies (see plate 54), which were always opalescent. Marbles in lines two and three are called pinchers by some collectors. It has been reported that they are found in games made in the 60's in Japan. At first glance they appear to be two-pontil marbles. They have been called transitions by a few collectors. They are usually of the peewee size, seldom found in larger or ⁵⁄₈" sizes. Line four are the off-white marbles made by Master Made, often mistaken for the Akro Agate moonies. They are not made of opalescent glass.

What are transitions? Not all noted authors agree, and knowledgeable collectors are even further apart. Are they Early American handmade marbles? Or are they hand fed machine made marbles (made before the invention of the automatic fed machines), or both? How do you tell the difference? These are only a few of the questions I have in regard to "transitions." Examining marbles in collections has helped but it has not answered a lot of questions. One very fine collection contained one marble obviously made in the 60's with an imperfection refferred to as a pontil. One collection of transition marbles contained only what I believed to be American handmade, another only early machine made. One knowledgeable collector stated the transition period was a very short time. A noted glass authority stated there never was a marble machine used in the Christensen Agate factory. Could she have meant an automatic fed marble machine? And the controversy goes on. But doesn't that add interest to marble collecting?

Plate 34: American handmade called horizontal swirls, very rare. Transitions? From the collection of Brian Estepp.

Plate 35: Early machine-made marbles. Transitions?

Plate 36: An exceptionally fine shooter size group. American handmade? Or early machine made? Does it really matter? From the collection of Bud Brawnlich.

28

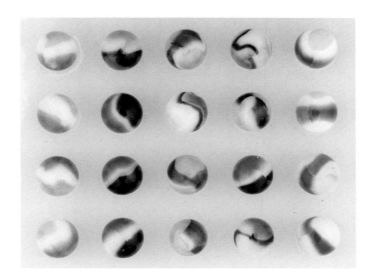

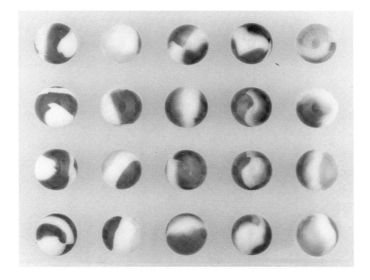

Plates 37 and 38: A variety of patched and ribboned over white matrix made by several different companies. They are plentiful and some are still being produced.

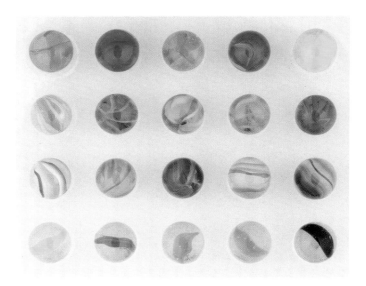

Plate 39: Line one is the U.S. No. I cat-eye. Lines two and three are the beautiful American-made No. 2 cat-eye. Line four is the original cat-eye or banana made by the Peltier Glass Company.

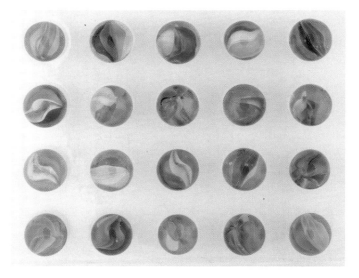

Plate 40: Foreign-made multi-color cat-eyes made in both Japan and Mexico.

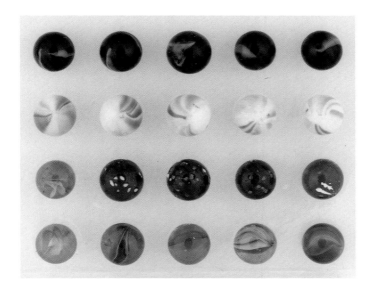

Plate 4I: New foreign-made marbles.

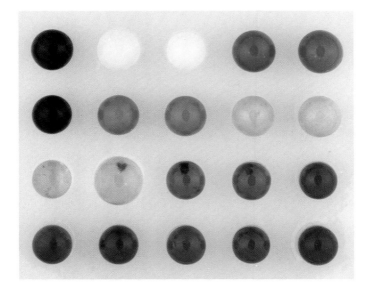

Plate 42: Lines one and two are the opaque Chinese Checker marbles. Lines three and four are the new transparent marbles called clearies and puries.

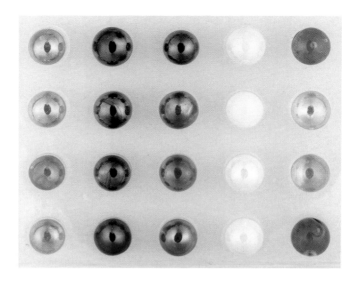

Plate 43: These are new iridescent marbles (also called carnival glass) now being produced in the United States and Mexico.

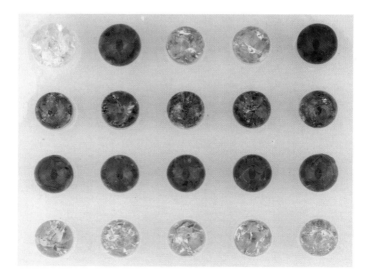

Plate 44: Crackle glass: Since back in the 1940's, perfectly good marbles have been placed in ovens at home and heated to a high temperature. They are then taken out and sprinkled with cold water, causing them to crack in this manner. These are sometimes mistaken for micas by new collectors.

Plate 45: Here is a mixed collection of less expensive marbles. Some have names that I know, but most I do not know. I asked the help of a self-proclaimed expert as to the names and/or maker. His reply was, "Junk. Just junk. All junk." Well, I don't agree. They may not be expensive but each one is a beautiful specimen in its own way. The point is, beautiful marbles can still be collected without spending a lot of money.

Plate 46: Here is a collection a little more expensive than plate 45, but still not a marble in the box that I would value at more than $2.00.

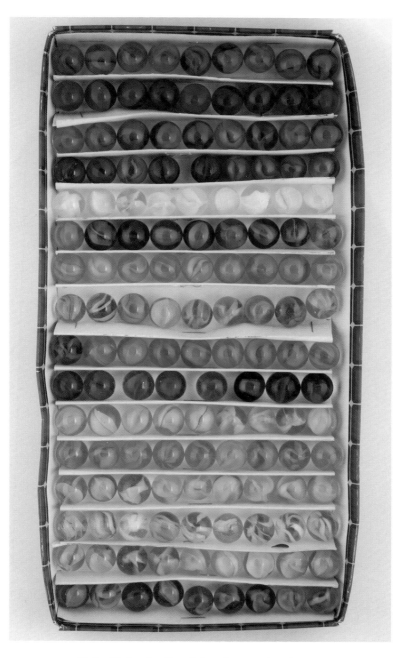

Plate 47: A collection of American-made cat-eyes.

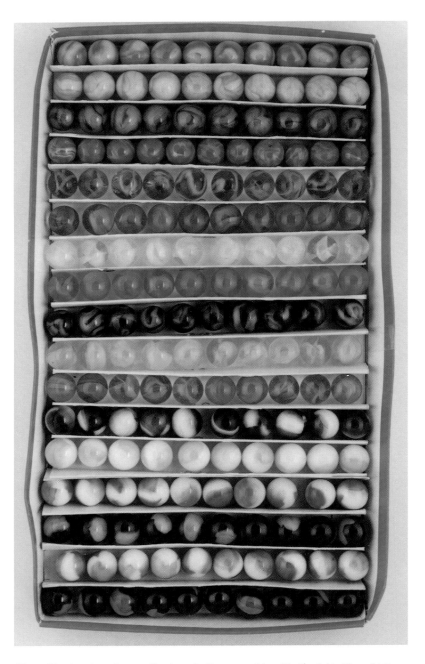

Plate 48: And here is a collection of all new marbles. That's right. I bought them all within the past year and I never paid more than five cents each for any of them. At that price, I have a total of less than $17.00 invested in this complete collection.

Notice the marbles in plates 45 through 48 are displayed in shoebox lids with strips of thin cardboard separating the rows. Though these got a little banged up transporting them to the photographer, it is a good and inexpensive way to show and store them.

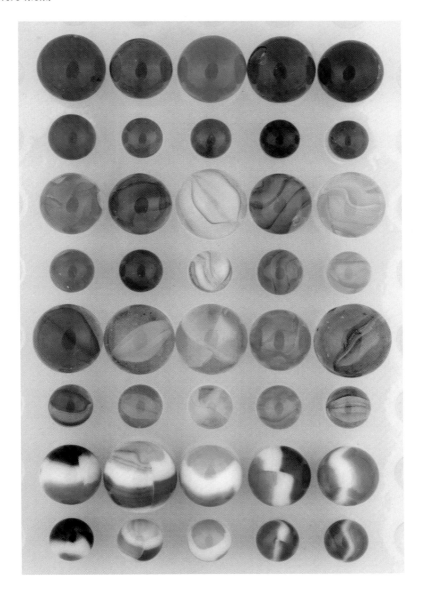

Plate 49: Two examples, alike except for the size. This is an interesting way to collect marbles. I first saw marbles collected in this manner about ten years ago by Helen Grainger of Mason, Michigan.

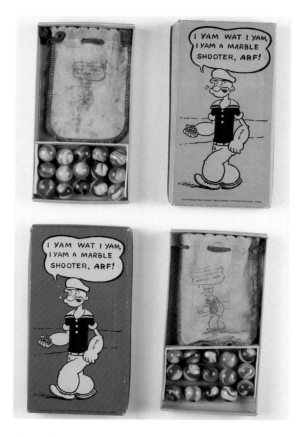

Plate 50 and 51: Popeyes in boxes. Though these boxes are alike, we show all four to get a better idea of the variety of Popeyes. Courtesy Jim and Louise O'Connell.

Plate 52: Akro Imperials. Courtesy Jim and Louise O'Connell.

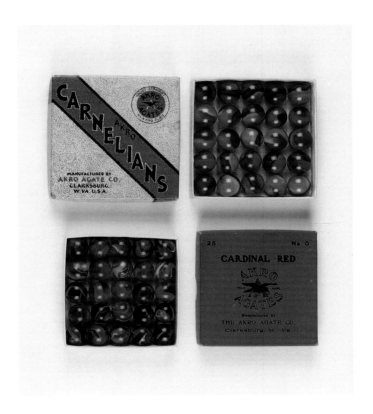

Plate 53: Akro Carnelians and Akro Cardinal Reds.

39

Plate 54: Akro moonies. It is believed that some of the marbles in this box may not be original. Courtesy Jim and Louise O'Connell.

Plate 55: Akro agates with marble bag. Courtesy Jim and Louise O'Connell.

Plate 56: Akro Agate marbles and bag. Note sparklers in low left hand corner. Also the two yellow and red marbles referred to as pumpkins. Logo on box says "Akro Agates Shoot Straight As A Kro Flies." Courtesy Jim and Louise O'Connell.

Plate 57: Akro Agate moss agates. Courtesy Jim and Louise O'Connell.

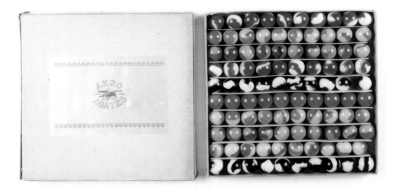

Plate 58: Akro Agate opaque corkscrews. Courtesy Jim and Louise O'Connell.

42

Plate 59: Akro Agate opaque corkscrews with bag. Courtesy Jim and Louise O'Connell.

Plate 60: Akro Agate Click game. Courtesy Jim and Louise O'Connell.

Plate 6l: Akro Agate moss agates. Courtesy Gary and Sally Dolly.

Plate 62: Akro Agate sparklers. Courtesy Gary and Sally Dolly.

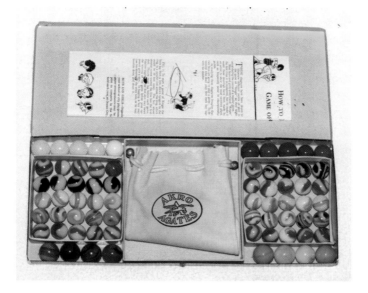

Plate 63: Akro Agate with bag in metal box. Courtesy Gary and Sally Dolly.

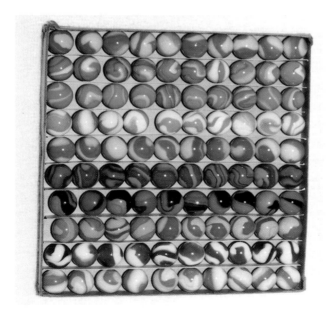

Plate 64: Akro Agate box of 100 corkscrews. Courtesy Gary and Sally Dolly.

Plate 65: Akro Agate box of 50 tri-color corkscrews. Courtesy Gary and Sally Dolly.

Plate 66: Akro Agate marbles with Kullerbubbel Gum promotion packet. Note large shooter corkscrew in center of picture. Courtesy Gary and Sally Dolly.

Plate 67: Akro Agate slag marbles in graduating sizes in each color. Courtesy Gary and Sally Dolly.

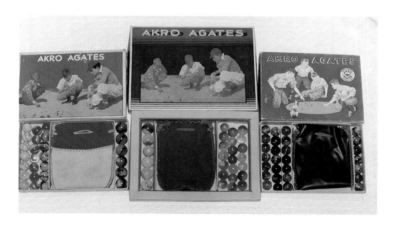

Plate 68: Three versions of Akro Agate boxes with bag. One features oxbloods; another, moss agates; the third, slags. Courtesy Gary and Sally Dolly.

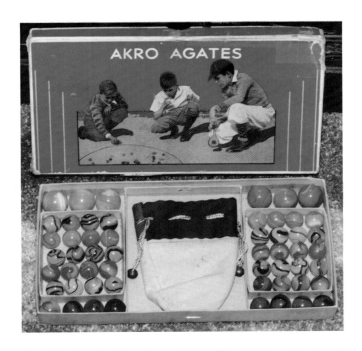

Plate 69: Another Akro Agate with bag. Note the large shooters at the back of box, also the oxbloods. Courtesy Gary and Sally Dolly.

Plate 70: Another Akro Agate with bag. This box contains moss agates in the large shooter size. Courtesy Gary and Sally Dolly.

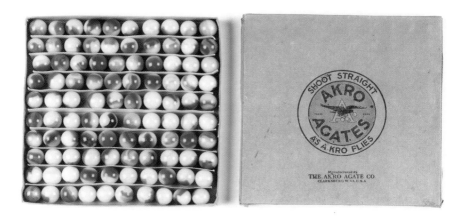

Plate 71: Akro Agate box of 100 with the patched and ribboned marbles. Courtesy Jim and Louise O'Connell.

Plate 72: Another Akro Agate box of 100. Courtesy Jim and Louise O'Connell.

Plate 73: More of the same type of marbles in a different box. Courtesy Jim and Louise O'Connell.

Plate 74: Christensen Agate slags. Courtesy Brian Estepp.

Plate 75: More Christensen Agate slags, size No. 4. Courtesy Gary and Sally Dolly.

Plate 76: Christensen Agate slags, size No. 5. Courtesy Gary and Sally Dolly.

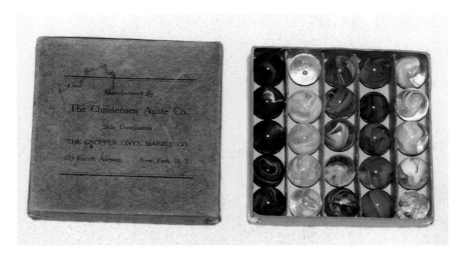

Plate 77: Christensen Agate slags, size No. 4, in a different box. Courtesy Gary and Sally Dolly.

Plate 78: Christensen Agate slags with one row of red and white flames. Courtesy Gary and Sally Dolly.

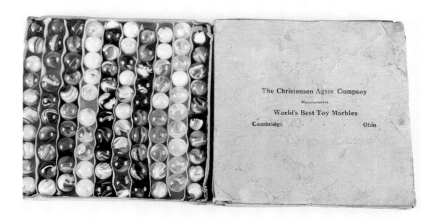

Plate 79: A box of 100 Christensen Agate slags showing some unusual colors. Courtesy of Brian Estepp.

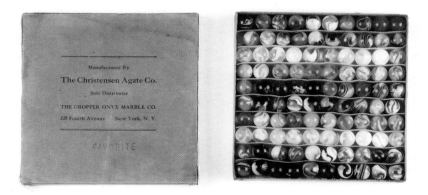

Plate 80: Another box of 100 Christensen Agate slags. Courtesy of Jim and Louise O'Connell.

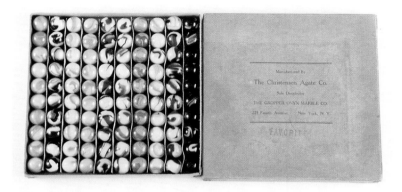

Plate 81: Christensen Agate box of 100 opaques. Courtesy of Brian Estepp.

Plate 82: Christensen Agate Company's American Agates. Courtesy of Brian Estepp.

Plate 83: A box of No. 6 Christensen Agate slags with one row of American Agates. Courtesy of Brian Estepp.

Plate 84: A partial box of Christensen Agate
peewees. Courtesy of Brian Estepp.

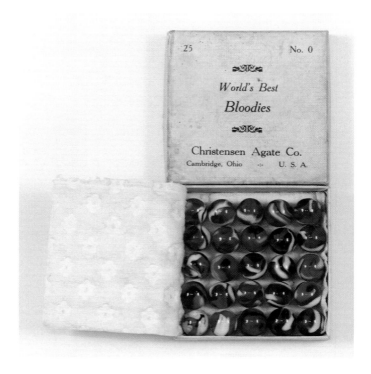

Plate 85: Christensen Agate World's Best Bloodies. Courtesy of Brian Estepp.

Plate 86: Christensen Agate World's Best Guineas. Courtesy of Brian Estepp.

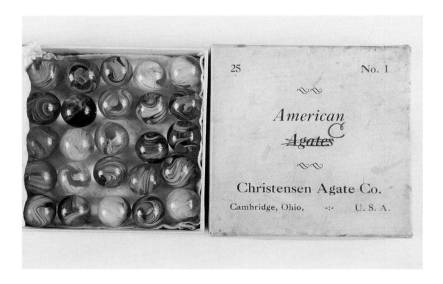

Plate 87: Christensen Agate box marked American Agates with the Agates marked out and a "C" added. These are now called cyclones. They are also known as cobras, but it is believed the "C" originally stood for clearies. These are very rare marbles and few have been found, the majority of those found were in the boxes. Courtesy of Brian Estepp.

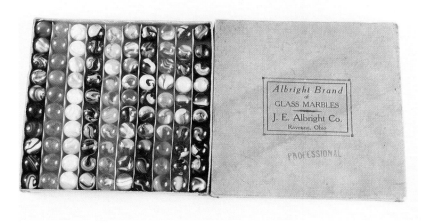

Plate 88: Albright brand. We believe this to be a Christensen Agate box with the stamp of a distributor added. The words "Cambridge, Ohio" appear on the side of the box. Courtesy of Brian Estepp.

Plate 89: Albright brand paper label applied over Christensen Agate stamp. Courtesy of Brian Estepp.

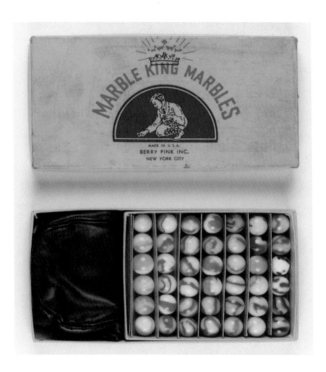

Plate 90: Marble King, 42 marbles with bag. Courtesy Jim and Louise O'Connell.

Plate 91: Master Made Marble Co. moss agates. Courtesy Jim and Louise O'Connell.

Plate 92: Master Made Marble Co. Chicago Worlds Fair 1933 Century of Progress. Marbles are moss agates and solid colors. Courtesy Jim and Louise O'Connell.

Plate 93: Another version of the Chicago Worlds Fair Master Made boxes and bags. Courtesy Jim and Louise O'Connell.

Plate 94: Master Made Marbles.

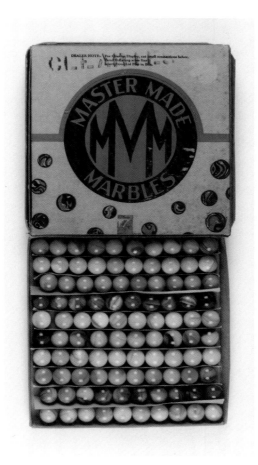

Plate 95: A box of Master Made Marbles.
Courtesy Jim and Louise O'Connell.

Plate 96: These are the white marbles made by Master Made that look like the Akro Agate moonies but are not opalescent. Courtesy Jim and Louise O'Connell.

Plate 97: Master Marble Shooter Set. Courtesy Jim and Louise O'Connell.

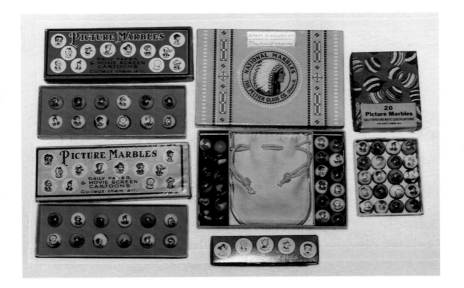

Plate 98: Peltier Picture Marbles, now called comics. On the left are two boxes of 12 marbles each, one red, the other yellow. The top center box contains 12 picture marbles and bag, with other marbles on the left. Lower center is a box of five picture marbles. On the right is a box of picture marbles. Courtesy of Gary and Sally Dolly.

Plate 99: Vitro Agate Company box containing marbles similar to some of the Akro Agates shown earlier. Courtesy Jim and Louise O'Connell.

Plate 100: A red box with no company name.

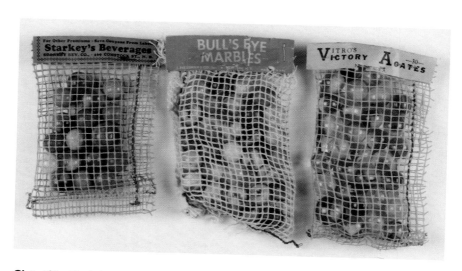

Plate 101: Mesh bags of marbles. Packaging material used helps us date the marbles. This type was in common use until after World War II. Courtesy Jim and Louise O'Connell.

Plate 102: Mesh bags of marbles. Courtesy Jim and Louise O'Connell.

Plate 103: Plastic bags of marbles. This type of plastic packaging material was not available until the early 1950's.

72

Plate 104: Latest packaging material has children's age advisements.

Contemporary Art Glass

The popularity of marble collecting has increased dramatically in the past ten years. One indication is the number of artists now producing art glass marbles.

Marble-mania, the newsletter of MCSA, volume 34, April, 1984, stated: "We know of three makers of handmade marbles at this time," and asked for information on others.

The next issue listed 12 names with many question marks as to addresses. Now more than 30 artists are known to be turning out some of the most fantastic marbles imaginable... even more beautiful than the antique marbles. But we must remember that the workers who were making the old marbles (mostly in Germany) were making children's toys, retailing for seldom more than 35 cents each, whereas today's art glass marbles start for as much as $20.00 and go into the hundreds.

We are often asked, "Where can these marbles be purchased?" Therefore, for your convenience, we are including that information in this book. On the following pages are those makers who were good enough to send pictures and/or answer our letter of inquiry.

Harry Boyer
207 N. State Street
P.O. Box 733
Harbor Springs, MI 49740
616/526-6359

Steven Maslach
44 Industrial Way
Greenbridge, CA 94904
415/924-2310

Mark Matthews
State Route 2
P.O. Box 332
Archibold, OH 43502
419/446-2541

David P. Salazar
545 Bellevue Street
Santa Cruz, CA 95060
408/423-2877

Douglas Sweet
Route 2 Box 99B
Lowell, OH 45744
614/896-2418

This is the label from the box of 12 comic strip marbles that is now being sold.

COMIC STRIP MARBLES

BY BENNETT   12   CAMBRIDGE, OHIO

Harold D. Bennett
506 S. 9th Street
Cambridge, OH 43725
614/432-3045

Dudley F. Giberson, Jr.
P.O. Box 202
Warner, NH 03278
603/456-3569

Jody Fine
1800 - 4th Street
Berkeley, CA 94710
415/845-4270

Josh Simpson
Frank Williams Road
Shelburne Falls, MA 01370
413/625-6145

If you are searching for a small number of new marbles of a certain size or color for your game boards or any other reason, we suggest The Marble Man.

THE MARBLE MAN   Gameboards
&
Marbles

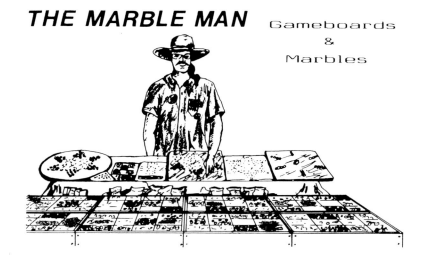

The Marble Man
P. O. Box 4302
Woodbridge, VA 22194

Price Guide

You may ask of me: "Do you consider yourself an expert?"

"No," is my reply, although I am so considered by some who I know to be much more worthy than I. It is to some of these persons that I have turned for advice for this book and price guide.

Keep in mind that I do not have a hoard of a certain type of marble that I want to sell, so I have no reason to want to run the prices up; and I am certainly not interested in buying your marbles at a low percentage of what they are actually worth. Therefore, the basis for this price guide is this basic and simple rule: if I owned all of the marbles pictured herein at this time and they were for sale, this is the price that I would ask for them.

Prices quoted are for ⅝" size marbles unless it is obvious from the photograph that they are of a different size.

Plate 3

	A	B	C	D	E
1)	$35.00	$35.00	$25.00	$25.00	$25.00
2)	$25.00	$25.00	$35.00	$25.00	$25.00
3)	$25.00	$25.00	$25.00	$25.00	$25.00
4)	$25.00	$25.00	$25.00	$25.00	$25.00

Plate 4

	A	B	C	D	E
1)	$25.00	$25.00	$25.00	$25.00	$25.00
2)	$25.00	$25.00	$25.00	$25.00	$25.00
3)	$25.00	$25.00	$25.00	$25.00	$25.00
4)	$100.00	$100.00	$60.00	$60.00	$60.00

Plate 5

	A	B	C	D	E
1)	$20.00	$20.00	$20.00	$20.00	$20.00
2)	$25.00	$25.00	$25.00	$25.00	$25.00
3)	$25.00	$25.00	$25.00	$15.00	$35.00
4)	$10.00	$10.00	$10.00	$10.00	$25.00

Plate 6

	A	B	C	D	E
1)	$40.00	$40.00	$40.00	$40.00	$40.00
2)	$40.00	$40.00	$40.00	$40.00	$40.00
3)	$20.00	$20.00	$20.00	$20.00	$20.00
4)	$40.00	$40.00	$40.00	$40.00	$40.00

Plate 7

	A	B	C	D	E
1)	$30.00	$30.00	$100.00	$100.00	$80.00
2)	$80.00	$80.00	$80.00	$80.00	$60.00
3)	$100.00	$100.00	$100.00	$100.00	$60.00
4)	$60.00	$60.00	$60.00	$60.00	$60.00

Plate 8

	A	B	C	D	E
1)	$80.00	$100.00	$100.00	$100.00	$80.00
2)	$120.00	$120.00	$120.00	$120.00	$120.00
3)	$120.00	$120.00	$120.00	$120.00	$120.00
4)	$120.00	$120.00	$120.00	$120.00	$120.00

Plate 9

	A	B	C	D	E
1)	$120.00	$120.00	$120.00	$120.00	$120.00
2)	$80.00	$80.00	$100.00	$100.00	$100.00
3)	$60.00	$60.00	$120.00	$120.00	$60.00
4)	$100.00	$80.00	$120.00	$80.00	$120.00

Plate 10

$15.00 each

Plate 11

	A	B	C	D	E
1)	$25.00	$25.00	$25.00	$25.00	$25.00
2)	$25.00	$25.00	$25.00	$25.00	$25.00
3)	$15.00	$15.00	$15.00	$15.00	$15.00
4)	$25.00	$25.00	$25.00	$25.00	$25.00

Plate 12

$15.00 each

Plate 13

$4.00 each

Plate 14

$25.00 each

Plate 15

	A	B	C	D	E
1)	$75.00	$75.00	$75.00	$75.00	$75.00
2)	$175.00	$175.00	$200.00	$250.00	$250.00
3)	$250.00	$250.00	$200.00	$250.00	$150.00
4)	$75.00	$100.00	$150.00	$150.00	$150.00

Plate 16

	A	B	C	D	E
1)	$20.00	$10.00	$20.00	$25.00	$45.00
2)	$20.00	$20.00	$10.00	$30.00	$20.00
3)	$15.00	$20.00	$20.00	$25.00	$35.00
4)	$15.00	$15.00	$40.00	$30.00	$20.00

Plate 17

	A	B	C	D	E
1)	$250.00	$300.00	$300.00	$300.00	$300.00
2)	$30.00	$30.00	$10.00	$15.00	$10.00
3)	$10.00	$10.00	$10.00	$15.00	$25.00
4)	$60.00	$60.00	$10.00	$25.00	$10.00

Plate 18

	A	B	C	D	E
1)	$250.00	$300.00	$400.00	$300.00	$250.00
2)	$40.00	$40.00	$30.00	$20.00	$20.00
3)	$30.00	$200.00	$200.00	$200.00	$200.00
4)	$40.00	$40.00	$40.00	$40.00	$40.00

Plate 19

	A	B	C	D	E	F
1)	$350.00	$350.00	$250.00	$300.00	$300.00	$300.00
2)	$400.00	$400.00	$300.00	$300.00	$350.00	$350.00
3)	$400.00	$400.00	$400.00	$400.00	$400.00	$400.00
4)	$200.00	$250.00	$200.00	$300.00	$200.00	$200.00
5)	$250.00	$250.00	$200.00	$200.00	$250.00	$200.00

Plate 20

	A	B	C	D	E
1)	$15.00	$20.00	$10.00	$20.00	$20.00
2)	$20.00	$25.00	$25.00	$25.00	$25.00
3)	$10.00	$10.00	$10.00	$10.00	$10.00

Plate 21

	A	B	C	D
1)	$100.00	$100.00	$100.00	$85.00
2)	$100.00	$150.00	$120.00	$120.00
3)	$85.00	$100.00	$100.00	$100.00

Plate 22

	A	B	C	D	E
1)	$80.00	$80.00	$150.00	$80.00	$80.00
2)	$60.00	$60.00	$120.00	$60.00	$60.00
3)	$60.00	$60.00	$120.00	$60.00	$60.00
4)	$60.00	$60.00	$120.00	$60.00	$60.00

Plate 23

	A	B	C	D	E
1)	$60.00	$60.00	$60.00	$60.00	$60.00
2)	$60.00	$60.00	$60.00	$60.00	$60.00
3)	$60.00	$60.00	$60.00	$60.00	$60.00
4)	$200.00	$60.00	$80.00	$80.00	$60.00

Plate 24, 25, & 26

Not enough sales to indicate a trend. Estimate $3.00 average.

Plate 27

	A	B	C	D	E
1)	$15.00	$10.00	$15.00	$10.00	$10.00
2)	$5.00	$5.00	$10.00	$5.00	$5.00
3)	$5.00	$5.00	$10.00	$5.00	$5.00
4)	$5.00	$5.00	$5.00	$5.00	$5.00

Plate 28

	A	B	C	D	E
1)	$40.00	$40.00	$40.00	$40.00	$40.00
2)	$20.00	$20.00	$20.00	$20.00	$20.00
3)	$20.00	$20.00	$10.00	$10.00	$10.00
4)	$10.00	$10.00	$10.00	$10.00	$10.00

Plate 29

$1.00 each

Plate 30

.50¢ each.

Plate 31

$1.00 each.

Plate 32

$1.00 each

Plate 33

	A	B	C	D	E
1)	$3.00	$3.00	$3.00	$3.00	$3.00
2)	$1.00	$1.00	$1.00	$1.00	$1.00
3)	$1.00	$1.00	$1.00	$1.00	$1.00
4)	$1.00	$1.00	$1.00	$1.00	$1.00

Plate 34

No price available

Plate 35

	A	B	C	D	E
1)	$40.00	$60.00	$40.00	$40.00	$60.00
2)	$60.00	$60.00	$60.00	$60.00	$60.00
3)	$120.00	$60.00	$120.00	$120.00	$120.00
4)	$40.00	$40.00	$40.00	$40.00	$40.00

Plate 36

No price available.

Plate 37 & 38

.25¢ each

Plate 39

.10¢ to $1.00

Plates 40 – 44

$.05 each

Plate 45

.25¢ to $1.00

Plate 46

$1.00 to $5.00

Plate 47

.05¢ to .50¢ each

Plate 48

.05¢ each

Plate 49

.05¢ to $1.00

Boxes and Bags

Plate 50

Popeyes ---------------------------------$1,100.00 each box

Plate 51

Popeyes --------------------------------$1,100.00 each box

Plate 52

Imperials ------------------------------------$600.00 each

Plate 53

Carnelians ---$700.00
Cardinal Reds -------------------------------------$275.00

Plate 54

Moonie ---$550.00

Plate 55

Akro Agate, w/marble bag, picture of boys -----Avg. $550.00

Plate 56

Akro Agate, shoot straight, w/bag--------------------$350.00

Plate 57

Akro Agate, 100 Moss Agates ----------------------$600.00

Plate 58

Akro Agate, 100 Opaque Corkscrews ---------------$550.00

Plate 59

Akro Agate, Opaque Corkscrews w/bag ------------$1,500.00

Plate 60

Akro Agate, Click game w/100 opaque C.S. ---------$350.00

Plate 61

Akro Agate, 100 Moss Agates ----------------------$350.00

Plate 62

100 sparklers ------------------------------------$2,000.00

Plate 63

Akro Agate, metal box -----------------------------$300.00

Plate 64

100 Opaque, C.S.- some tri-color --------------------$750.00

Plate 65

50 tri-color Akro Agate ----------------------------$850.00

Plate 66

Bubblegum box ----------------------------------$2,500.00

Plate 67

30 Akro Agate slags -----------------------------$550.00

Plate 68

Akro Agate, w/bag, picture of boys--------------Left $750.00
Center $500.00
Right $1,200.00

Plate 69

Akro Agate, ox-blood w/bag, picture of boys ---------$750.00

Plate 70

Akro Agate, Moss Agate w/bag and large shooters --$750.00

Plate 71

Akro Agate, late -----------------------------------$200.00

Plate 72

another late ---------------------------------------$200.00

Plate 73

smaller deeper box----------------------------------$400.00

Plate 74

Slag -- box $900.00

Plate 75

Slag size #4--$900.00

Plate 76

Slag size #5--$1,100.00

Plate 77

Slag size #4--$900.00

Plate 78

Slags & Flames ------------------------------------$1,750.00

Plate 79

Slags--$900.00

Plate 80

Slags--$900.00

Plate 81

Opaques --$1,000.00

Plate 82

Christensen Agate's American Agates-------------$1,200.00

Plate 83

#6 Slag & American Agates-----------------------$1,500.00

Plate 84

Christensen Agate--------------------------------$1,500.00

Plate 85

Bloodies---$600.00

Plate 86

Guineas--$8,000.00

Plate 87

Cyclones --$12,500.00

Plate 88

Albright --$1,500.00

Plate 89

Albright --$2,000.00

Plate 90

M. King, 42 marbles w/bag ------------------------$325.00

Plate 91

Master Made, Moss Agate, about 75 marbles--------$225.00

Plate 92

Worlds Fair ---$700.00

Plate 93

Worlds Fair ---$700.00

Plate 94

Mastermade ---$15.00

Plate 95

100 Master Made late --------------------------------$150.00

Plate 96

Master Made White-----------------------------------$425.00

Plate 97

M. M. Shooter Set ------------------------------------$500.00

Plate 98

Picture Marbles (red box of 12) --------------------$1,500.00
Picture Marbles (yellow box of 12) -----------------$1,500.00
National Marbles Boxed Set w/bag-----------------$2,750.00
Box of 5 Comics Marbles ---------------------------$750.00
Picture Marbles Box of 20------------------------$1,850.00

Plate 99

Vitro Agate ---$475.00

Plate 100

Red Box ---$10.00

Plate 101

Advertising mesh bag----------------------------each $20.00

Plate 102

Mesh Bag ---------------------------------------each $20.00

Plate 103

Plastic Bag --------------------------------------each $5.00

Plate 104

Late Bag --each $2.00

Other Books
By Everett Grist

Antique & Collectible Marbles
Revised Third Edition
5½ x 8½, 96 pages, PB, $9.95

Covered Animal Dishes
8½ x 11, 120 pages, PB, $14.95

Advertising Playing Cards
8½ x 11, 232 pages, PB, $16.95

Collectible Aluminum
8½ x 11, 160 pages, PB, $16.95

Big Book of Marbles
8½ x 11, 143 pages, HB, $19.95